SPORTS
BASLET
NBA

MEMPHIS
GRIZZLIES

by Marty Gitlin

Published by ABDO Publishing Company, 8000 West 78th Street, Edina, Minnesota 55439. Copyright © 2012 by Abdo Consulting Group, Inc. International copyrights reserved in all countries. No part of this book may be reproduced in any form without written permission from the publisher. SportsZone™ is a trademark and logo of ABDO Publishing Company.

Printed in the United States of America,
North Mankato, Minnesota
062011
092011

Editor: Chrös McDougall
Copy Editor: Anna Comstock
Series design: Christa Schneider
Cover production: Craig Hinton
Interior production: Carol Castro

Photo Credits: Jim Mone/AP Images, cover; Nick Procaylo/AP Images, 1; Adrian Wyld/AP Images, 4, 43 (top); Mark Humphrey/AP Images, 6, 33, 36, 43 (middle), 47; Eric Gay/AP Images, 9; Chuck Stoody/AP Images, 10, 14, 20, 42 (top and middle); Elaine Thompson/AP Images, 13; Ann Heisenfelt/AP Images, 17; Steve Yeater/AP Images, 18; Rich Pedroncelli/AP Images, 23; Jim Weber/AP Images, 25; Tony Gutierrez/AP Images, 26, 38, 42 (bottom); Paul Connors/AP Images, 29; Mark Weber/AP Images, 30; Nikki Boertman/AP Images, 34; Matt Slocum/AP Images, 41, 43 (bottom); David Zalubowski/AP Images, 44

Library of Congress Cataloging-in-Publication Data
Gitlin, Marty.
  Memphis grizzlies / by Marty Gitlin.
     p. cm. -- (Inside the NBA)
  Includes index.
  ISBN 978-1-61783-162-1
  1. Memphis Grizzlies (Basketball team)--History--Juvenile literature. I. Title.
  GV885.52.M46G58 2011
  796.323--dc23
                              2011019410

TABLE OF CONTENTS

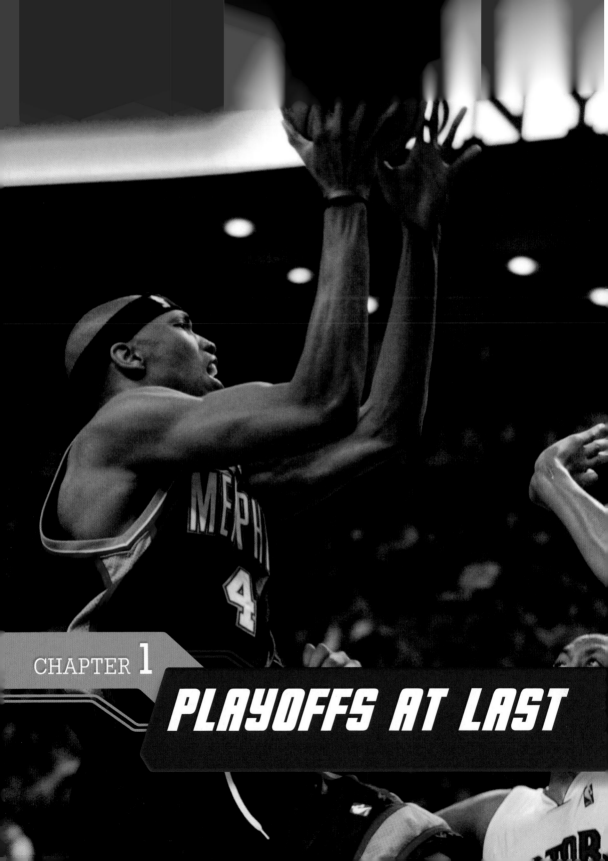

CHAPTER 1

PLAYOFFS AT LAST

The Memphis Grizzlies clung to an 82–78 lead. But they were playing in Toronto, where the crowd was screaming for a Raptors victory. And there were still nearly three minutes left to play.

Grizzlies point guard Jason Williams then did something about the loud Raptors fans. He quieted the crowd by launching a three-pointer that dropped perfectly through the net. Then he did it again. Suddenly the Grizzlies were ahead 88–78. It was all over but the celebration. On March 28, 2004, the Grizzlies qualified for the playoffs for the first time in franchise history.

The Grizzlies had been one of the worst teams in the National Basketball Association (NBA) since they joined as an expansion team in 1995. They were awful as the Vancouver Grizzlies through 2001.

The Grizzlies' Stromile Swift puts up a shot against the Toronto Raptors on March 28, 2004. With a win, the Grizzlies qualified for the playoffs for the first time.

NBA Commissioner David Stern, *right*, presents Grizzlies coach Hubie Brown with the 2004 NBA Coach of the Year Award.

And they were still awful after moving to Memphis. They had finished the previous season with a 28–54 record. And that had been their best mark ever.

"It's a great turnaround for the franchise," said Grizzlies star center Pau Gasol after the win over the Raptors. "We've surprised ourselves. I can't believe where we are at this point. It's just wonderful."

Early on, the 2003–04 season appeared on its way to being another losing one for the Grizzlies. They entered 2004 with a 15–17 record. But they suddenly caught fire. The Grizzlies won 34 of their 43 games during one three-month period.

Hot and Cold

When the Grizzlies got hot during the 2003–04 season, they remained hot. They embarked on two seven-game winning streaks from February 28 to April 2. They won eight consecutive games in January and six straight games in early December. The Grizzlies did run hot and cold, though. The eight-game tear came just after they had lost seven in a row.

The Grizzlies' success was thanks to an overall team effort. Eight Grizzlies players scored at least 8.5 points per game during the regular season. Gasol was their best player, leading them with averages of 17.7 points and 7.7 rebounds per game. But he received plenty of help from Williams, forwards James Posey, Stromile Swift, and Shane Battier, guards Bonzi Wells and Mike Miller, and center Lorenzen Wright.

Much of the credit, however, belonged to veteran coach Hubie Brown. He took over the team after a horrible start in 2002–03. And the Grizzlies grew from there. They became one of the few teams in league history to lose 50 games in one season and win 50 the next. After the 2003–04 season, Brown was named NBA Coach of the Year.

There was a problem, though. The Grizzlies played in the strong Western Conference. They had blossomed into a fine team, but they were not at the level of perennial title contenders such as the Los Angeles Lakers and the San Antonio Spurs. Entering the playoffs, the Grizzlies were seeded sixth in the West.

And there was another problem. The Grizzlies ended the regular season by losing six of their last seven games. Their momentum was gone. They needed to be playing their best when the playoffs began—but they were playing their worst.

Their poor play showed when the Grizzlies started their first playoff series against the powerful Spurs. The Grizzlies struggled to score. In two losses to start the series, they averaged a meager 72 points per game. They only made about one-third of their shots, including only 24 percent of their three-point attempts.

The Grizzlies knew they had to win Game 3 in Memphis to have any chance at upsetting the Spurs. More than 19,000 fans packed the arena they called the Pyramid. And they chanted for the coach.

"Hubie, Hubie, Hubie!" they called out. Brown replied by blowing kisses to the crowd. He later said it was "one of the greatest nights of my life."

It would have been greater had the Grizzlies won—and they almost did. They led 57–50 at halftime, but scored just 36

Defensive Stoppers

One of the reasons the Grizzlies improved so much in 2003–04 was their superior defense. They were one of the worst defensive teams in the NBA during the 2002–03 season, surrendering 100.7 points per game to place 27th out of 29 teams in the league. But the following year they gave up just 94.3 points per game to rank 15th.

points the rest of the game. They still had a chance to win, but Miller missed a three-pointer at the buzzer.

The Grizzlies' playoff inexperience showed with the game on the line. They lost the ball in four of their last five possessions. But even with his team on the verge of elimination, Miller held out hope for a victory in Game 4.

"We don't want to get swept," he said. "So we have to come out here with guns blazing on Sunday and play as hard as we did tonight."

Grizzlies forward Pau Gasol shoots over San Antonio Spurs defenders during the 2004 playoffs. The Spurs swept the Grizzlies in four games.

It was not to be, however, as the Spurs completed the sweep in Game 4. Fans in Memphis still had reason to be excited. After so many losing seasons, the Grizzlies had finally shown that they could win, and they had a strong core of young players coming back the next season.

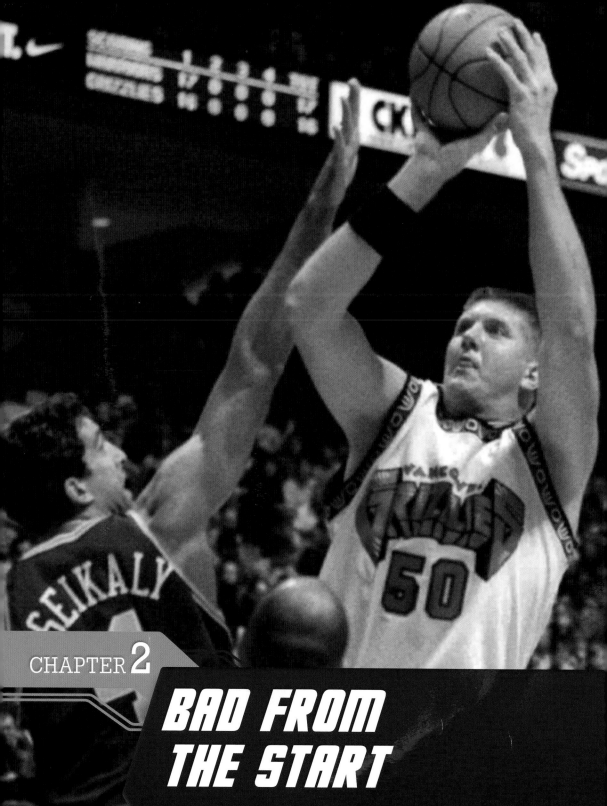

CHAPTER 2

BAD FROM THE START

he NBA had expanded several times since it began in 1949. But it had never expanded beyond the borders of the United States. That is, until 1995. For the 1995–96 season, the NBA added two Canadian teams: the Vancouver Grizzlies and the Toronto Raptors.

The NBA officially granted Vancouver a team on April 27, 1994. Owner Arthur Griffiths was no stranger to professional sports—he already owned the National Hockey League's Vancouver Canucks. His new team got off to a surprising start. The Grizzlies won their first game on the road against the Portland

What's in a Name?

When the NBA awarded a team to Vancouver, the team decided to call itself the Grizzlies because grizzly bears are native to British Columbia—the Canadian province in which Vancouver resides. Some have wondered why the nickname did not change when the team moved to Memphis. After all, there are no grizzly bears in Tennessee.

Grizzlies center Bryant "Big Country" Reeves goes up for a shot against the Golden State Warriors in 1995. Reeves played for the Grizzlies from 1995 to 2001.

Trail Blazers, and their second game at home against the Minnesota Timberwolves.

But the honeymoon quickly ended. The Grizzlies lost their next 19 games. And that was not even their longest losing streak that season. The Grizzlies dropped 23 in a row from mid-February to early April. That was the longest single-season losing streak in NBA history until the Cleveland Cavaliers lost 26 in 2010–11. The Grizzlies finished the year with a woeful 15–67 record.

One-Game Wonder

One player rose to the occasion when the Grizzlies played their first game ever in 1995. And that was center Benoit Benjamin. He led the team with 29 points and 13 rebounds in a 92–80 victory over the Portland Trail Blazers. But he did not score more than 22 points in any game during the rest of the season. And he only once pulled down more than 13 rebounds.

Even as the losses mounted, Grizzlies veteran guard Byron Scott spoke proudly about his team during the losing streak.

"If you're just going to pack it in, you're not showing any discipline or heart or courage," he said. "Even though we've lost 21 straight, we've never packed it in. We've played everybody hard. That's something I'm very proud of."

Most expansion teams struggle during their first season and gradually improve. Grizzlies coach Brian Winters and general manager Stu Jackson knew they needed to select a premier college player in the 1996 draft to follow that trend. They did just that by getting forward Shareef Abdur-Rahim. He quickly blossomed into the Grizzlies' best player during his rookie season. Abdur-Rahim led the team in scoring and was second in rebounding.

Greg Anthony is fouled by a Seattle SuperSonics player during a 1995 game. Anthony led the Grizzlies in scoring in their first season.

His strong performances did not help in the team win column, though. After an 8–35 start, Jackson fired Winters and named himself the new coach. But Jackson fared no better. The Grizzlies lost 15 straight down the stretch. They finished the season averaging fewer than 90 points per game and were second to last in the NBA in scoring. And they actually got worse in their second season under Jackson, winning only 14 games.

Brian Hill took over as the Grizzlies' coach for the 1997–98 season. Hill had enjoyed

Grizzlies forward Shareef Abdur-Rahim drives to the basket against the Los Angeles Clippers during a 1996 game.

previous success, coaching the Orlando Magic to the NBA Finals just three seasons earlier. The Grizzlies improved offensively in their third season but collapsed on defense. They gave up 104 points per game.

It was hard to win with such lousy defense. During one stretch, they went 6–41. In the midst of that streak, they gave up at least 101 points in 15 consecutive games.

The Grizzlies boasted strong inside play with

Big Country

The Grizzlies wanted a talented young center to start their franchise with in 1995. So they made burly 7-footer Bryant "Big Country" Reeves their first pick in the NBA Draft. The selection brought mixed results. Reeves never became an All-Star, but he averaged more than 16 points and approximately eight rebounds per game during his second and third seasons. However, his career was cut short by injuries. Most believe he was not worth the $11 million per year he received from the Grizzlies.

Abdur-Rahim and center Bryant "Big Country" Reeves. Abdur-Rahim averaged 22.3 points per game during the 1997–98 season. But the team had little scoring elsewhere.

The Grizzlies were worse than ever during the 1998–99 season, which was shortened by a work stoppage. They finished with an 8–42 record and lost 36 of their last 40 games. For the first time in their history, they placed among the bottom three NBA teams in both offense and defense. The addition of rookie point guard Mike Bibby helped, but the Grizzlies were again lacking in talent.

The brief love affair the Grizzlies had with their fans began to wear off. Attendance dropped at General Motors Place, their home arena. Griffiths tried to sell the team to Bill Laurie, who made it no secret that he planned to move it to St. Louis, Missouri. But the NBA rejected the sale. So Griffiths instead sold the team to Chicago businessman Michael Heisley in January 2000. He said he would not move the team.

It was a worrying move. Some believe Heisley had no intention of keeping the Grizzlies in Vancouver. After all, why would an owner from a major US city want to keep a

DRAFT DISASTER

With the second pick in the 1999 NBA Draft, the Grizzlies selected talented guard Steve Francis. But Francis did not want to go to Vancouver. He said it was too far from his Maryland home and he worried that he would not get enough publicity by playing in western Canada. The Grizzlies were forced to trade Francis to the Houston Rockets for several players and draft picks. Meanwhile, Francis blossomed to become NBA Co-Rookie of the Year with the Rockets.

Many people were upset with Francis's attitude and with the Grizzlies. "What is it with the preparation of the Grizzlies in this area?" a local columnist wrote. "When they talk to these kids, don't they . . . ask the kid or his agent or his grandmother whether he would mind playing in Vancouver?" Fans pelted Francis with tomatoes and eggs when the Rockets played in Vancouver that season.

failing team in Canada? But Heisley claimed he did.

Times remained tough for the Grizzlies in Vancouver, though. Heisley had only owned the team for a month and they had already lost 12 consecutive games. Hill was replaced by another new coach in Lionel Hollins, but nothing seemed to work. The Grizzlies finished the 1999–2000 season with a 22–60 record. There were more empty seats in the arena than ever before— only two of the 29 NBA teams attracted fewer fans that season. The future of professional basketball in Vancouver was looking very dim.

Grizzlies point guard Mike Bibby dribbles around Minnesota Timberwolves guard Terrell Brandon during a 1999 game. Bibby played for the Grizzlies from 1999 to 2001.

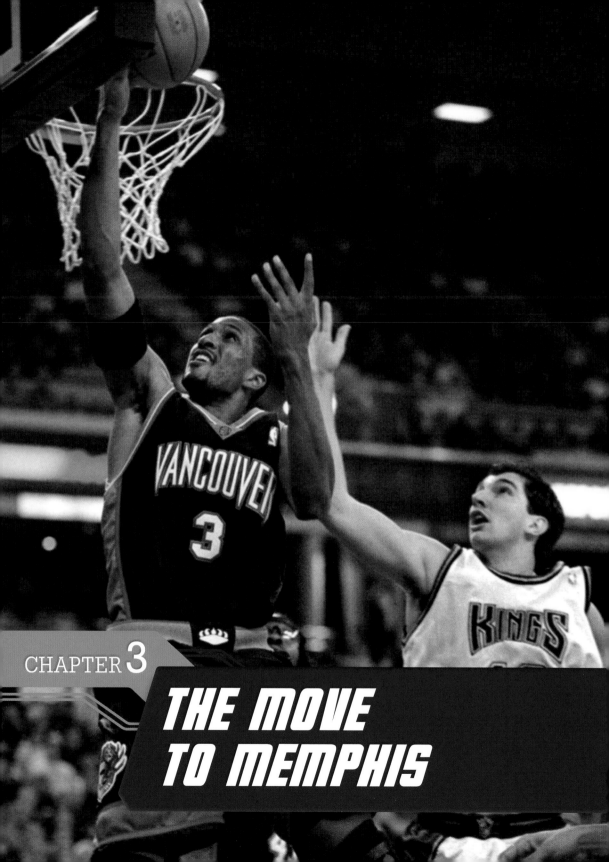

CHAPTER 3

THE MOVE TO MEMPHIS

After five losing seasons, the Grizzlies were getting desperate. They had already hired and fired four coaches by the time Sidney Lowe took over at the beginning of the 2000–01 season.

Lowe had not been a head coach since a short stint with the Minnesota Timberwolves in the early 1990s. But he quickly discovered what the other Grizzlies coaches had also found out—the team did not have enough talent to thrive.

The Grizzlies were encouraged when they won four of their first five games. But they went on to lose 21 of their next 25, and 23 of their last 28 that season. The Grizzlies were again one of the worst offensive and defensive teams in the NBA. The final result was a 23–59 record.

The team also averaged fewer than 14,000 fans per

The Grizzlies' Shareef Abdur-Rahim makes a layup against the Sacramento Kings in a 2001 game. Abdur-Rahim led the Grizzlies with 20.5 points per game in 2000–01.

Bryant "Big Country" Reeves (50) attempts to win the tip off during one of the Grizzlies' final games in Vancouver in February 2001.

game. The NBA average was 16,784 fans per game. The few fans that did come to Grizzlies games learned on July 3, 2001, that they would not get another chance to attend one. That was when the NBA approved owner Michael Heisley's plan to move the franchise to Memphis, Tennessee. He had lost an estimated $40–50 million since taking ownership of the team in 2000.

Many refused to blame the fans or the players for the Grizzlies' disastrous stint in Vancouver. Jay Triano, who served as the Grizzlies radio announcer since their beginning, blamed those who ran the team. And he predicted more failures in Memphis.

"Now Memphis is going to have to go through the same sorry [stuff] that we had to in Vancouver," he said. "Those moves are [terrible]. They had two legitimate stars in [Shareef Abdur-Rahim and Mike Bibby], and they didn't get value back."

Indeed, the Grizzlies had traded their two best players—Abdur-Rahim and Bibby—after the 2000–01 season. But Triano was wrong about the results of those deals. In return for Abdur-Rahim, the Grizzlies received forward/center Pau Gasol. He developed into per-haps the team's best player ever. And the trade of Bibby brought point guard Jason Williams to the team. He paired with Gasol to turn the Grizzlies into winners.

The fans of Memphis were thrilled to have the Grizzlies.

Big Night at the Pyramid

There was no doubt about the highlight of the Grizzlies' first season in Memphis. It came on the night of December 21, 2001, when they beat the defending NBA champion Los Angeles Lakers, 114–108. The hero in that game was Brevin Knight. The backup point guard made all but one of his 10 shots and finished with 20 points.

They had yearned for a major-league sports team for many years. In order to get the team, city officials had to promise they would build it a new arena. After much discussion, they did just that. The FedExForum was constructed while the Grizzlies played their first three seasons at the Pyramid.

If the Grizzlies and their fans assumed the move would mean more wins, they would be disappointed. Gasol recorded 17.6 points and 8.9 rebounds per game to win the NBA Rookie

Tough Luck

Because of their bad record, the Grizzlies earned the second pick in the 2003 NBA Draft. If only they had been able to use it. When the team was still in Vancouver, it traded that draft pick to the Detroit Pistons for forward Otis Thorpe, who ended up only playing a little more than half a season with the Grizzlies. Had they instead kept that second pick, the Grizzlies could have chosen a future NBA superstar, such as Carmelo Anthony or Dwyane Wade.

of the Year Award in 2001–02. Williams averaged eight assists per game to lead the team. And swingman Shane Battier played stellar defense. But for the second straight season, the Grizzlies finished with a measly 23–59 record.

When the Grizzlies lost their first eight games of the 2002–03 season, a frustrated Lowe resigned and was replaced by coach Hubie Brown. Although Brown had coached the Kentucky Colonels to the 1974–75 American Basketball Association (ABA) title, he had not coached in the NBA for 15 years. But team president and general manager Jerry West believed Brown could finally turn around the franchise.

"I feel very confident we got a guy here who will be the ultimate teacher," West said. "Our players are going to be in for a shock . . . a positive shock. The thing that surprised me most is that [Brown] sounds like a teenager ready for his first date. When I look at Hubie and his knowledge of the game, I just truly believe it was something he wanted to do again."

Brown might have soon had second thoughts. His team lost 10 of its next 12 games to fall to 2–18. But suddenly the Grizzlies showed marked improvement for the first time in team history. They won almost half of their games in

Grizzlies point guard Jason Williams prepares to shoot against the Sacramento Kings during a 2001 game.

December. They embarked on a six-game winning streak in March. And they finished the season with a franchise-best 28 victories.

The new coach had his team scoring consistently. They placed eighth in the NBA in scoring by averaging 97.5 points per game. During one

A GOOD CHOICE

The Grizzlies needed a coach with a history of success after Sidney Lowe resigned in 2002. So they turned to Hubie Brown. It was a good choice. Brown guided the Kentucky Colonels to the ABA title during his first year as coach in 1975. He then latched on as coach of the Atlanta Hawks after the ABA folded in 1976. He won NBA Coach of the Year honors in 1977–78, and guided the Hawks to three straight playoff appearances. He later led the New York Knicks into the playoffs twice.

Brown became one of the most well-known NBA analysts on TV broadcasts in between his coaching stints. He was the lead analyst for CBS starting in 1988. He later moved on to cable network TNT. Brown was nominated for a Sports Emmy award in both 1994 and 1999. He later worked on NBA broadcasts for ABC. Following his stint with the Grizzlies, Brown was elected into the Basketball Hall of Fame in 2005.

stretch in February and March, the Grizzlies scored at least 100 points in 13 of 18 games. Nine players averaged nearly 10 points per game or more.

The Grizzlies finally had reason to be optimistic as they headed into the 2003–04 season. And after Brown and Gasol led the charge to the first playoff berth in franchise history, the challenge was clear. They had to do it again as they moved to the brand new FedExForum. And this time, they needed to contend for an NBA championship.

Grizzlies forward Pau Gasol dribbles the ball past a Los Angeles Clippers defender during a 2003 game. Gasol averaged 19 points and 8.8 rebounds per game that year.

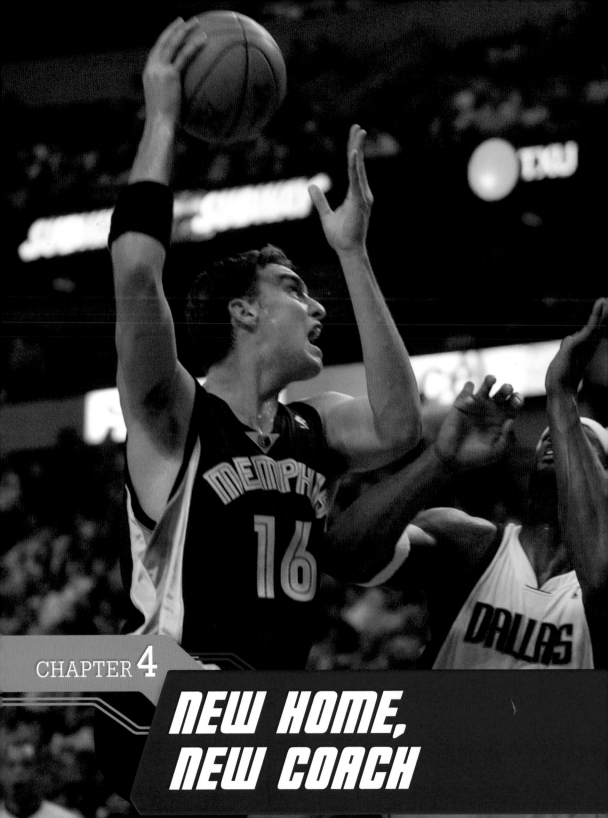

CHAPTER 4

NEW HOME, NEW COACH

Everything seemed to be looking up for the Grizzlies when the 2004–05 season began. They returned with virtually the same team that had earned the first playoff berth in franchise history one year earlier. They were opening the new FedExForum. And they still had Hubie Brown as their coach. But not for long.

After just 12 games, the 71-year-old Brown felt overwhelmed by the strain of the job and abruptly retired. After four consecutive losses under interim coach Lionel Hollins, veteran Mike Fratello took over. Fratello had earned a reputation as a good coach. But he was also known for slowing the pace of the game. His teams walked the ball up and down the floor and kept scores low. Many players and fans believed that meant boring basketball, but his teams generally won.

Pau Gasol puts up a hook shot during a 2004 game against the Dallas Mavericks.

MIKE FRATELLO

Mike Fratello is known as much for his work as an NBA analyst on TV as he is for coaching. He was nicknamed the "Czar of the Tele-strator" by NBC broadcasting partner Marv Albert. He earned the title for his ability to explain strategies of the game by drawing on a screen seen by the audience. Fratello served as an analyst on NBC, TNT, and the NBA Network in between coaching gigs.

He is still considered one of the better coaches in recent NBA history. His teams won consistently, but not in the playoffs. His emphasis on defense helped the Atlanta Hawks to five straight winning seasons. He also guided the Cleveland Cavaliers to five consecutive winning records. But Fratello's teams were just 20–42 in the playoffs. He lost 20 of the last 22 playoff games he coached, including all eight with the Grizzlies.

The Grizzlies often won under Fratello. And they did it with defense. From late November to April 10 they surrendered 100 or more points just seven times in 60 games, and they compiled a 39–21 record during that stretch. Fratello was named Western Conference Coach of the Month in January, when the Grizzles went 12–3.

The Grizzlies needed every one of those victories to remain in playoff contention. They did not clinch the eighth and final postseason spot in the Western Conference until the last week of the season. And all that earned them was a series against the high-flying Phoenix Suns.

The first-round showdown featured teams with contrasting styles. The Suns raced up and down the court. They led the NBA in scoring at 110

Grizzlies point guard Jason Williams gets in a defensive position during a 2005 playoff game against the Phoenix Suns.

points per game. The Grizzlies, on the other hand, placed fourth in the league in defense. Their job was to slow down the Suns.

But they could not do it. For the second straight year, the Grizzlies were swept in four straight games in the first round of the playoffs. They allowed the Suns to score nearly 114

Balanced Bunch

The defensive intensity coach Mike Fratello required of his players meant that they needed frequent breaks. Nobody played more than 32 minutes per game during the 2004–05 season. Even top player Pau Gasol averaged 16 minutes of rest during the 48-minute games. The strategy resulted in scoring balance. Ten players scored at least 7.7 points per game that year.

The Grizzlies' Shane Battier was known for his tough defense and scrappy play. He played in Memphis from 2001 to 2006 and returned in 2011.

points per game. And the Grizzlies were not all getting along. Guard Bonzi Wells was angry about what he believed to be a lack of playing time. Fratello responded by benching him in Games 2 and 4. And the coach did not feel like his team played with enough emotion until the 123–115 loss in Game 4.

"I thought I saw for the first time a genuine pull for each other," Fratello said after the series-clinching defeat. "If you're going to go out, you want to go out swinging, and I thought the guys did that."

The Grizzlies became the first NBA team to lose their first eight playoff games. So they overhauled their roster after the season. Jason Williams and James Posey were traded to the Miami Heat for guard Eddie Jones. Wells was sent to the Sacramento Kings in a trade for guard Bobby Jackson. And center Stromile Swift signed a free-agent contract with the Houston Rockets.

The Grizzlies still had Pau Gasol and Shane Battier. They also boasted Mike Miller, who could make shots from just about anywhere on the court. But most importantly, they had a stifling defense. The 2005–06

Lockdown D

The Grizzlies surrendered fewer than 70 points in five of their first 34 games in 2005–06. They gave up 100 or more points only 12 times all year, and they surrendered the fewest baskets in the NBA. The Grizzlies were especially strong defending three-point shots. Opponents made just over 33 percent of their three-point attempts that season. The Grizzlies ranked second in the league in that category.

Grizzlies gave up the fewest points in the NBA at 88.5 per game.

The Grizzlies finished the regular season at 49–33 and fifth in the Western Conference. They were playing their best basketball heading into the playoffs, having won 15 of their last 19 games. Most believed they would lose to the fourth-seeded Dallas Mavericks in the first round of the playoffs. However, this appeared to be the year that the Grizzlies might at least win one playoff game.

It was not. The Grizzlies were swept in four games for the third straight season. Their 12-game playoff losing streak was the longest in NBA history.

The most painful defeat came in Game 3, after the Grizzlies had lost the first two games badly in Dallas. The Grizzlies owned a 78–75 lead with 15 seconds remaining. But then Mavericks superstar Dirk Nowitzki hit a three-pointer to tie it. And Grizzlies guard Chucky Atkins missed a layup at the buzzer that could have given his team the victory.

The game went into overtime. The Mavericks made their first four shots in the extra period and won, 94–89. The Grizzlies had scored just 43 points in the second half and overtime combined.

"It's one of the toughest losses, and it's very disappointing right now," Gasol said. "Right now, it's extremely painful."

It would get more painful when his team was clobbered in Game 4. They had been swept out of the playoffs for the third consecutive year. It had become obvious that the Grizzlies were not good enough to contend for an NBA title. It was time to rebuild. And that would mean going back to their losing ways.

Grizzlies forward Pau Gasol struggles to get by a Dallas Mavericks defender during their 2006 playoff series.

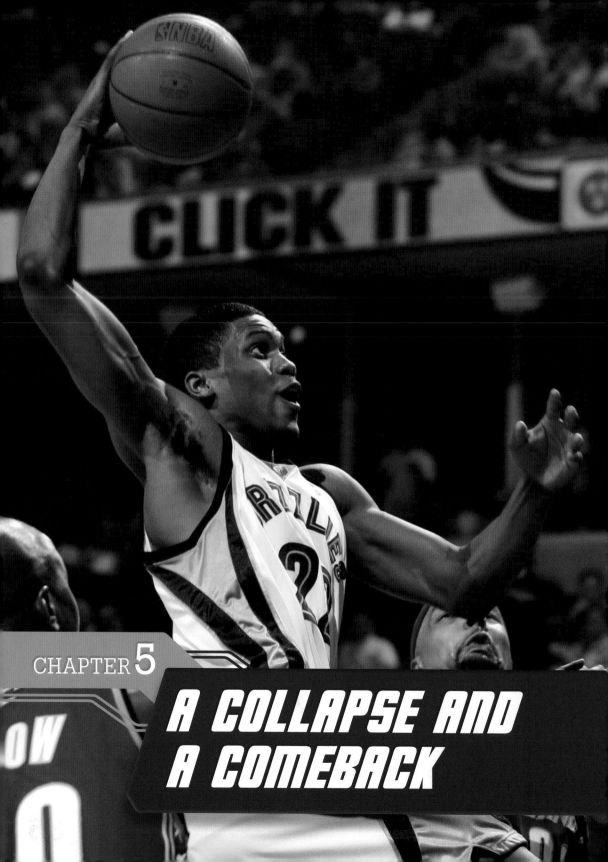

CHAPTER 5

A COLLAPSE AND A COMEBACK

There was one player that the Grizzlies could not afford to lose. But they lost him for 22 games in 2006. Then they lost him for good in 2008. That player was Pau Gasol.

Gasol missed most of the first two months of the 2006–07 season with a broken foot. The Grizzlies had already traded veterans Shane Battier and Lorenzen Wright. Rookie Rudy Gay showed promise but was only 20 years old. He was not ready to replace the production lost by the trades and the Gasol injury.

The result was disastrous. The Grizzlies won just six of their first 30 games. Even the trademark defense of coach Mike Fratello began to collapse. After the team gave up 100 or more points in five straight losses, he was fired.

Team president and general manager Jerry West believed that the players were

Grizzlies rookie forward Rudy Gay leaps through the air for a slam dunk during the 2006–07 season.

Grizzlies president of basketball operations Jerry West endured a difficult 2006–07 season.

Empty Seats

The fans in Memphis have not responded to the Grizzlies as well as the team had hoped when it moved there from Vancouver. The Grizzlies have been near the bottom in NBA attendance rankings every year since the move. They were twenty-fourth in the league or lower in attendance in all but one of their first nine seasons in Memphis. Since 2006, they ranked in the bottom three all four years. They placed dead last in attendance in both 2006–07 and 2008–09.

unhappy with Fratello and his slow-down style of play.

"Our players simply had lost confidence," he said. " . . . It was a trust factor, and I don't think there was any question there was a lot of unrest in our locker room."

West surprised many by replacing Fratello with Director of Player Personnel Tony Barone. Barone had no head coaching experience. But West planned to have him in that position only through that season. West wanted Barone to adopt a faster pace on the floor. West also believed that through coaching, Barone would gain a better understanding of what the team needed, which would help him become a better personnel director.

The Grizzlies played no better under Barone than they did for Fratello. They never won more than three games in a row for the rest of the season. They finished with a miserable 22–60 record.

There was also another problem. A month after Fratello was fired, Gasol asked to be traded. He wanted to play for a team that had a chance to win a title. It had become apparent that the Grizzlies were not going to contend for quite some time.

That was enough for West, who quit after the season. New general manager Chris Wallace and coach Marc Iavaroni—Barone's replacement—would be forced to deal with the unhappy Gasol. The Grizzlies stumbled to start the next year and never recovered. Wallace realized the team needed to get rid of Gasol's high salary. He also wanted to trade for players whose contracts were running out, which would free up money to spend on rebuilding the team.

Jerry West

Perhaps the most recognized person affiliated with the Grizzlies was President of Basketball Operations Jerry West. He had been a star guard with the Los Angeles Lakers during the 1960s and early 1970s. Many consider him to be one of the best players in NBA history. West didn't tolerate losing in Memphis. He took over in 2002 and turned the Grizzlies into winners. Starting in 2003–04, they made the playoffs for three consecutive years.

The Grizzlies added rookie O. J. Mayo (32) on a draft-day trade before the 2008–09 season in hopes that he could help turn the team around.

Gasol got his wish on February 1, 2008, by getting traded to the Los Angeles Lakers. He helped them win NBA titles in 2009 and 2010. In return, the Grizzlies received four players and two first-round draft picks.

"I hate to use the word [rebuilding]," Wallace said after completing the deal. "But I think I'm a realist. We're a 13-win team so don't kid yourself. Don't sugarcoat it. We've got some interesting pieces, but we're a 13-win team. In that situation you've got to look and make moves. It's time to try a new course."

The new course had to work better than the old one. The Grizzlies were on their way to a second straight 22–60 season. They won just one game in February and lost six of their first seven games in March. Wallace understood that they had to make wise draft picks. He had to stock the roster with young talent to rebuild the franchise.

The first step was trading picks with the Minnesota Timberwolves in the 2008 draft. That allowed the Grizzlies to acquire explosive guard O. J. Mayo. He sometimes allowed his temper to get the best of him, but he displayed great scoring ability, averaging 18.5 points per game as a rookie. Gay was also emerging as a solid player. He led the team that same year by scoring 18.9 points per game.

Iavaroni did not last long enough to be a part of the team's gradual improvement. He was fired in the midst of a 12-game losing streak in early 2009. Memphis finished the 2008–09 season with a 24–58 record.

The young team added veteran forward Zach Randolph in a trade that off-season. He was the strong force inside that the Grizzlies had lacked since trading Gasol. He combined with Gasol's younger brother, Marc Gasol, to give the Grizzlies a strong inside presence during the 2009–10 season. Memphis lost eight of its first nine games in that season, but by late January the team was 25–19 and contending for the playoffs. Although the Grizzlies finished 40–42 and just outside of the playoffs, the new core of players showed potential.

After an 8–14 start to 2010–11, the Grizzlies turned it around. Randolph averaged a team-high 20.1 points and 12.2 rebounds per game as Memphis finished 46–36. That was good enough to get the Grizzlies back into the playoffs for the first time since 2006.

As the eighth seed in the Western Conference, however,

the Grizzlies were big underdogs against the powerful San Antonio Spurs. But behind a combined 49 points and 23 rebounds from Gasol and Randolph, Memphis shocked the Spurs 101–98 to win Game 1. It was the team's first playoff victory ever.

Still, few gave Memphis a shot at winning the series, especially after it lost Game 2 93–87. But the younger, energetic Grizzlies did just that, beating the aging Spurs in six games. Then Memphis won the first game in its second-round series against another young team, the Oklahoma City Thunder. It was a tight, back-and-forth series. Game 3 went to overtime and Game 4 went to triple overtime.

It all came down to Game 7. Despite 18 points and six assists from point guard Mike Conley, the Grizzlies fell 105–90. After the game, even some Grizzlies players had a hard time being too upset. After all, they had exceeded almost everybody's expectations with their historic playoff run. And with so many young players, the 2011 postseason was only the beginning.

In 2011, center Marc Gasol did something his brother Pau Gasol could not: lead the Grizzlies out of the first round of the playoffs.

TIMELINE

1994
The NBA announces on April 27 that it is adding a franchise in Vancouver.

1995
The Grizzlies win at Portland, 92–80, on November 3 in their first-ever game. They win their second game as well before losing 19 in a row.

1996
The Grizzlies drop their 23rd straight game on April 2 to establish the longest single-season losing streak in NBA history. The Cleveland Cavaliers broke the streak in 2010–11.

1996
The Grizzlies select forward Shareef Abdur-Rahim on June 26 with their first pick in the NBA draft. He would blossom into one of the top players in team history.

1997
Coach Brian Winters is fired on January 25 and replaced by Stu Jackson. Former Orlando coach Brian Hill takes over the team on June 27.

1999
The Grizzlies lose 36 of their last 40 games to end the season.

2000
Owner Arthur Griffiths sells the team on January 25 to Chicago businessman Michael Heisley, who vows to keep it in Vancouver. Sidney Lowe becomes the fifth Grizzlies coach in four years on June 1.

2001
After six losing seasons, the Grizzlies move to Memphis. They also deal Abdur-Rahim to the Los Angeles Clippers on June 27 in a trade that brings them Pau Gasol. Gasol would emerge as the best player in franchise history.

2002	Lowe resigns as coach on November 13 after the Grizzlies start the season with eight straight losses. Hubie Brown takes over and begins to turn the team around.
2004	The Grizzlies win 34 of their final 43 games to reach the playoffs for the first time. However, the San Antonio Spurs conclude a four-game playoff sweep of the Grizzlies on April 25 with a 110–97 victory.
2005	The Phoenix Suns finish off the second straight first-round playoff sweep of the Grizzlies on May 1.
2006	For the third straight year, the Grizzlies are swept in the first round of the playoffs. A 102–76 defeat to the Dallas Mavericks completes the sweep. Coach Mike Fratello is fired and replaced by Tony Barone on December 28 after a 6–24 start to the season.
2008	Gasol is traded to the Los Angeles Lakers on February 1 as the Grizzlies try to get younger and free up money to rebuild. The Grizzlies acquire guard O. J. Mayo, who was a first-round pick in the 2008 NBA draft.
2009	The Grizzlies acquire forward Zach Randolph on July 17 in a trade with the Los Angeles Clippers. Randolph emerges as the team's best player that season.
2011	The Grizzlies finish 46–36 and qualify for the playoffs for the first time since 2006. Then, behind Randolph, they upset the top-seeded Spurs in the first round, getting their first playoff game and series victory. The Grizzlies nearly defeat the Oklahoma City Thunder in the second round but lose in seven games.

QUICK STATS

FRANCHISE HISTORY

Vancouver Grizzlies (1995–2001)
Memphis Grizzlies (2001–)

NBA FINALS

None

DIVISION CHAMPIONSHIPS

None

PLAYOFF APPEARANCES

2004, 2005, 2006, 2011

KEY PLAYERS
(position[s]; years with team)

Shareef Abdur-Rahim
    (F; 1996–2001)
Shane Battier (F; 2001–06, 2011–)
Mike Bibby (G; 1998–2001)
Marc Gasol (C; 2008–)
Pau Gasol (F/C; 2001–08)
Rudy Gay (F; 2006–)
O. J. Mayo (G; 2008–)
Mike Miller (F; 2003–08)
Zach Randolph (F; 2009–)
Bryant Reeves (C; 1995–2001)
Jason Williams (G; 2001–05, 2011–)

KEY COACHES

Hubie Brown (2002–04):
    83–85; 0–4 (postseason)
Mike Fratello (2004–06):
    95–83; 0–8 (postseason)
Lionel Hollins (1999–2000; 2004–05;
    2008–):
    117–150; 7–6 (postseason)

HOME ARENAS

General Motors Place (1995–2001)
Pyramid Arena (2001–04)
FedExForum (2004–)

* All statistics through 2010–11 season

QUOTES AND ANECDOTES

"I intend to do everything in my power to make this franchise a success in Vancouver. Having an owner that is committed to this market is an important part." —New Grizzlies owner Michael Heisley after buying the franchise in 2000. He moved the team to Memphis the following year.

The Grizzlies play in a city with one of the finest college basketball programs in the country. The University of Memphis Tigers have produced 23 NBA players since the 1980s, including 2011 Most Valuable Player Derrick Rose, as well as Tyreke Evans, who was the Rookie of the Year in 2010. The success of former Tigers extends even further back. Forward Larry Kenon emerged in the 1970s to average 20 or more points per game for four straight years in San Antonio. Guard Penny Hardaway was drafted in 1993 and played in four NBA All-Star Games.

The Grizzlies selected Hasheem Thabeet with the second overall pick in the 2009 draft. They would quickly regret it. Thabeet averaged just three points per game as a rookie and was demoted to the NBA Developmental League in February, becoming the highest draft pick ever to be sent to that league as a rookie. The Grizzlies traded him to the Houston Rockets in February 2011.

"He'd rather talk basketball than eat. Every conversation I've had with him, it's about the game." —New York Knicks coach Lenny Wilkens on Hubie Brown after hearing that Brown had quit as coach of the Grizzlies in November 2004

How bad have the Grizzlies been since coming into existence in 1995? In their first 15 seasons in the NBA, the Grizzlies had 11 seasons in which they won 28 games or fewer.

GLOSSARY

assist

A pass that leads directly to a made basket.

attendance

The number of fans at a particular game or who come to watch a team play during a particular season.

contract

A binding agreement about, for example, years of commitment by a basketball player in exchange for a given salary.

draft

A system used by professional sports leagues to select new players in order to spread incoming talent among all teams. The NBA Draft is held each June.

expansion

In sports, the addition of a franchise or franchises to a league.

franchise

An entire sports organization, including the players, coaches, and staff.

general manager

The executive who is in charge of the team's overall operation. He or she hires and fires coaches, drafts players, and signs free agents.

interim

Temporarily holding a position until a permanent replacement is found.

overtime

A period in a basketball game that is played to determine a winner when the four quarters end in a tie.

postseason

The games in which the best teams play after the regular-season schedule has been completed.

rebound

To secure the basketball after a missed shot.

rookie

A first-year player in the NBA.

FOR MORE INFORMATION

Further Reading

Ballard, Chris. *The Art of a Beautiful Game: The Thinking Fan's Tour of the NBA*. New York: Simon & Schuster, 2009.

Lazenby, Roland. *Jerry West: The Life and Legend of a Basketball Icon*. New York: ESPN Books, 2010.

Simmons, Bill. *The Book of Basketball: The NBA According to the Sports Guy*. New York: Random House, 2009.

Web Links

To learn more about the Memphis Grizzlies, visit ABDO Publishing Company online at **www.abdopublishing.com**. Web sites about the Grizzlies are featured on our Book Links page. These links are routinely monitored and updated to provide the most current information available.

Places to Visit

FedExForum
191 Beale St
Memphis, TN 38103-3715
901-205-1234
www.fedexforum.com
This has been the Grizzlies' home arena since 2004. The team plays 41 regular season games here each year.

Naismith Memorial Basketball Hall of Fame
1000 West Columbus Avenue
Springfield, MA 01105
413-781-6500
www.hoophall.com
This hall of fame and museum highlights the greatest players and moments in the history of basketball. Former Grizzlies team president Jerry West is enshrined here.

Tennessee Sports Hall of Fame
501 Broadway
Nashville, TN 37203
615-242-4750
www.tshf.net
This hall of fame and museum features interactive games and exhibits for visitors to learn about sports and the greatest and most influential Tennessean sports people.

INDEX

About the Author

Marty Gitlin is a freelance writer based in Cleveland, Ohio. He has written more than 35 educational books, including many about sports. Gitlin has won more than 45 awards during his 25 years as a writer, including first place for general excellence from the Associated Press. He lives with his wife and three children.